SEVEN SPIRITS OF GOD

ANITA ANDREAS

MY WEBSITES:

TransformationinHisPresence.com
and
AnitaAndreas.com;

MY EMAIL:
anitaandreas8@gmail.com

MY BLOG:

BreakthroughHope.com

COVER ARTIST STATEMENT

Lynda Finch is an Artist and Teacher, who is based in Denver, Colorado. Her artworks are varied in subject matter, mediums and techniques. Lynda's goal is to show the beauty and wonder of God in creation. Her prophetic art portrays God's heart and His mysterious and majestic ways.

For more information, contact Lynda Finch via email at *lyndafinchart@gmail.com*

ISBN: 9780692096611

Endorsements

When I asked the LORD Jesus what He wanted to show me about His Seven Spirits of God message that was being released as a book by Anita Andreas, I saw a strong vision of hot steaming bread coming out of an oven. I felt He was saying it was His NOW Word, manna or bread from heaven for the body of Messiah.... that is coming out of the oven in His perfect timing!

Anita Andreas, the vessel through which the LORD delivered this message is a carrier of His presence and knows God's heart. She walks in a high level of discernment and integrity and walks in high authority in the Spirit for the things of God.

—CLAIRE ANGELA SESTER
Prophetic Evangelist
Bethel Church
Redding, California

Anita is a beautiful Isaiah 62:3 woman. She is a finely tuned and polished diadem in the hand of our God. Her passion to release people into personal encounter with Holy Spirit, Father God, or Jesus for themselves has forever changed my life and the many she has taught. She embodies the fruit of intimacy with Jesus. She reflects His faithfulness in every life situation, Father God's goodness and unconditional love. Anita's laid down love life of love has enabled her to hear from the Lord as He desires to speak to His children. Her pure heart reveals the Truth of His character with exceptional humility. I am honored to call her a friend and mentor who like God, never gives up on His children. I thank God for her in my life and every way I have learned to hear and follow Holy Spirit because of her.

—Nicol Runstrom
Int'l Missionary and Trainer
Prophetic / Healing Ministry
Bethel Church - Redding, California

Anita Andreas is a woman of sterling character in Jesus, Our Lord. Through the Holy spirit, she has a precision of a two-edged sword and is willing to spark truth in the hearts of those the Lord highlights to her. This is always blended with God's mercy and love.

I'm deeply touched by the fruit I see in the lives of whom Anita has poured into, helping them to hear more clearly from our Lord. It bears witness to the magnitude of what a mighty God we serve. I honor the work of her hands which are blessed by the LORD and the testimony of Jesus. She is a faithful friend of God and loyal to the lives of many including me.

—Mary Ann Hoffman
Father's Heart Ministry, New Zealand
Prophetic Intercessor/ Int'l Missionary
International House of Prayer, KC

Anita is a mighty prayer warrior in the Lord, used powerfully in the gifts of the Holy Spirit, a Seer as well as a vessel for healing people emotionally, mentally and physically. She is a dedicated faithful loyal and supportive friend to many, one who is known and can be trusted and relied on for prayer and wise counsel. Anita is very sensitive to the Holy Spirit, seeking His wisdom in all things, especially when ministering to others. The Lord's guidance and His direction, through the Holy Spirit are the main-stay of her ministry to the hurting and broken people including young children and teenagers. God uses

Anita in powerful ways, peoples' hearts change and they change. She helps people hear from God so they know it's the Lord who touched them and gave them their freedom and victory.

—JOSIE SANCHEZ
Deliverance and Healing Minister
Arvada, Colorado

Table of Contents

Preface i

Receiving the Message...i-v

OpeningPrayer...1

Walking Out the Flame of God's Light and Glory.................2

The Spirit of the Presence of the Lord Upon You.........8

Choice to Live in the Spirit....................................16

Waiting and Trusting in God....................................24

Kingdom Glory on the Earth.....................................32

Unity in the Spirit through Sound and Worship.................36

Loving each other to Sustain God's Glory......................42

Seven Spirits Shining In and Through You.....................48

Receiving His Grace through Trials.............................52

Humility and Dying to Self.....................................54

God's Love and Joy to Fight Your Battles......................56

Seeking God's Wisdom to Live God's Way........................62

Following God's Direction in All Things.......................68

Trusting God and Resting in Him...............................72

Walking in the Spirits of Wisdom and Understanding.......76

Inviting and Receiving the Spirits of Counsel and Might....86

God's Might to Walk in His Courage............................90

Intimacy with God to Walk in Your Calling....................96

Balancing Knowledge and Fear of the Lord....................108

All Honor and Glory to God to Bear Fruit....................120

Dedication...126

Preface

*T*his sacred message from Father God, Yahweh, Holy Spirit and Jesus Christ on the Seven Spirits of God bringing fuller revelation to Isaiah 11:2, Rev 1:4, Rev 4:5, and Rev 5:6 was given to me in March of 2008.

Though I asked the Lord about publication several times, I never felt released to share until now, this 2017. I submit this book with fear and trembling knowing clearly this was from Him and I dared not change a word from its original writing. It is His message and I am deeply grateful to be His messenger. It is intended to bless and edify the Body of Christ. All for His glory and honor.

Receiving the Message

It was March of 2008 driving on a country road near Denver Colorado. I desperately pumped the clutch of my '96 Subaru Outback, completely unable to shift gears. Slowing to a near halt, I glanced in the rearview mirror and gasped. Cars were bumper to bumper for a block behind me. I quickly pulled to the shoulder of the very narrow road, while grappling with my cell phone to contact a clutch repair service. The man on the phoneline was assuring me they would retrieve my car and repair it, as a police officer rolled up to assist me with a ride home. It all happened so fast.

Grateful to the state trooper, I arrived home only to realize that in my hurry, I'd left my prescription glasses on the dash. Further my phone was dead with no operable charger available. Dazed, I turned a slow circle in my living room, pondering this strange circumstance; no glasses, no phone and no car. Inquiring of the Lord, I asked, "Are you up to something, God?" Quickly I got the distinct impression that I was to take my computer, lie down on my couch, place my PC on my tummy and position my fingers on the keys, close my eyes and wait as a ready writer.

As I listened and responded, my fingers flew across the keys for the ensuing 2 ½ hours. The Holy Spirit opened with a lovely prayer that was more beautiful than I could ever remember praying evoking the Father, Jesus Christ and Holy Spirit. Knowing I was in safe and Holy Company, I relaxed and surrendered to the process. To my awe and astonishment, I could see God was conveying fresh revelation on the Seven Spirits of God, a subject for which I had little to no personal knowledge or understanding.

2 ½ hours later, I arose and read it slowly aloud. Touched by the beauty, power and purity of the message, I wept, sensing it may take years to fully unpack this gift from heaven. About 2/3 of the way through the read, however I panicked, "oh no!" I uttered. I came to a portion of the text where for 3 consecutive lines, the words were indiscernible. My mind raced. "what happened?" I had my eyes closed during the typing. I then realized my left hand must have moved slightly one set of keys over, creating a total unreadable mess. I knew I had no idea how to recall these lost lines of this powerful prophetic expression. After a weak attempt to paraphrase, I gave up. I had nothing.

Suddenly, I heard from the Spirit, "decode." So for the next hour, I laboriously decoded the 3 unreadable lines, "let's see if I hit this letter and my finger was supposed to be here, then it's really this letter....." And so on, until it all came together. Drawing a deep sigh of relief, thankfully the Word of the Lord was complete and in order. Later, upon reflecting, I smiled seeing God's hand in allowing this to happen that I would know this message was from Him and no one could take ownership but Him.

Since that writing to the point of this publication no word or phrase has ever, in any way, been changed or altered. It remains as the day of its writing with only the addition of scriptures, by a leading of the Holy Spirit, to support and enhance meditation and revelation.

Another beautiful confirmation of God's Hand upon this Word came several weeks later. A friend who hadn't known I had received a word on the Seven Spirits of God, arrived at my home with a gift in her hand. She explained that she had attended a prophetic conference in Houston, Texas and watched a brilliant artist, Lynda Finch, paint a stunning piece entitled, the Sevenfold Spirit of God and felt compelled by the Lord to purchase it for me. As I held this extraordinary piece of art depicting a menorah, engulfed in fire with seven colorful doves flying in and out of the lampstand and flames, I felt the Lord's orchestration of events to confirm His Word.

Just in this 2017, Lynda Finch and I have made contact. We each are amazed at the beautiful Hand of God in bringing us together for this work. Gratefully, she has given permission to present her "Sevenfold Spirit of God" as the cover of this book. I encourage you all to explore Lynda's many paintings displayed on her website and to consider bringing one of her magnificent treasures into your home which carry deep revelation and impartation of the Lord.

Opening Prayer

I surrender all to you Lord. I pray that you will now minister your Spirit through me to teach me and others who You are and whatever You desire to convey about Yourself through this message. My prayer is none of me and all of You for Your honor and glory oh dear sweet Jesus, Father God and precious Holy Spirit. Fall on me. Let your glory fall and open up a portal from your heavenly realm that the words that come forth are heavenly revelation of the unseen, the incomprehensible nature of the supernatural reality of Your being and Your exquisite unexplainable unknowable nature of love. I surrender my will. Thy will be done for Your name to reign, Your name above every name, Your ways above our ways. For Your purposes and plan to come forth and spread the seed for a mighty harvest that only You know how to reap. Amen and amen.

Walking Out the Flame of God's Light and Glory

MESSAGE FROM THE LORD

The seven lampstands burn the flame of My multifaceted heart within you, within each of you. I lit the flame of your existence that is Me and endued it into you as a gift to my creation the very day and hour you surrendered the old life to invite Me in. I burn in you and through you. That is what I meant when my prophet Isaiah and then My precious son Yeshua spoke: "Arise and shine, the glory of the Lord is risen upon you"[1]

---

1   Isaiah 60:1

Rev 4:5 And from the throne proceeded lightnings, thunderings and voices. Seven lamps of fire were burning before the throne, which are the Seven Spirits of God. NKJV

John 8,12:12 Then Jesus spoke to them again saying: I am the light of the world. He who follows Me shall not walk in darkness but have the light of life. NKJV

Message From the Lord

My Sevenfold Spirit is made manifest in and through you as you bow and worship Me and then walk out that worship by keeping your eyes, your vision on the Truth that sets you free, that you abide in Me and I abide in you. That you can exude Me, My heavenly countenance through your very face and being as you acknowledge that you are truly nothing without Me and nothing can separate you from Me nor Me from you.

John 15:4 Abide in Me and I in you. As the branch cannot bear fruit of itself unless it abide in the vine, so neither can you unless you abide in Me. NKJV

Matt 5:16 Let your light so shine before men that they may see your good works and glorify your Father in heaven. NKJV

Message From the Lord

Your light, My light within you can so shine before men that they will not see you but only see Me. As they gaze upon the face of your Witness to Me they will experience Me as they were meant to experience My sevenfold reality, the spirit of the presence of the Lord upon them as it is made manifest upon and through you.

Isaiah 11:2 The Spirit of the LORD will rest on Him, The Spirit of wisdom and understanding, The Spirit of counsel and might, The Spirit of knowledge and the fear of the LORD. NKJV

Rom 8:38-39 For I am persuaded that neither death nor life, nor angels, nor principalities nor powers, nor things present nor things to come, nor height nor depth, nor any created thing shall be able to separate us from the love of God which is Christ Jesus our Lord. NKJV

The Spirit of the Presence of the Lord Upon You

MESSAGE FROM THE LORD

So truly as Paul wrote, it is not you who lives but Christ who lives in you. That to die to this life is to gain True Life. Life of the presence of the Lord upon you, shining through, having surrendered all, gained all.

Gal 2:20 I have been crucified with Christ, Christ lives in me and the life which I now live in the flesh, I live by faith, the Son of God who loved me and gave Himself for me. NKJV

Phil 1:21 For to me, to live is Christ and to die is gain. NKJV

Message From the Lord

Let me habitate in and on you. Let me find that resting place in you. I search to and fro looking for a place to rest, hands and feet that are willing and are consecrated over to my purposes. My purposes to forgive, to show kindness, to care for one in need, to lift someone up in comfort and speak a timely encouraging word upon My prompting, to wait until My spirit leaps within you and My unction says "go now, stay now, speak now, remain silent now, love now, hold now, release now, embrace now."

John 14:15-17 "If you love Me, keep my commandments. And I will pray the Father and He will give you another Helper, that He may abide with you forever --- the Spirit of truth whom the world cannot receive because it neither sees Him nor knows Him, but you know Him, for He dwell with you and will be in you. NKJV

2 Chron 16:9 For the LORD runs to and fro throughout the whole earth to give strong support to those whose heart is blameless toward him. NKJV

Message From the Lord

What you do unto the least of your brothers you do unto Me. But not by works, yet in faith stepping out and acting upon My leading, because we are one and you move and be according to My will, shining My light through you into the dark and hidden places.

Matt 25:40 And the king will answer and say to them, "Assuredly I say to you, inasmuch as you did unto one of the least of these my brethren, you did it to Me. NKJV

Heb 11:6 But without faith it is impossible to please Him for he who comes to God must believe that He is, and that He is a rewarder of those who diligently seek Him. NKJV

Acts 17:28 for in Him we live and move and have our being, as also some of your own poets have said, "For we are also His offspring." NKJV

John 1:5 The light shines in the darkness, and the darkness has not overcome it. NIV

MESSAGE FROM THE LORD

Not for recognition, but in secret, that you only seek to please Me, the spirit of the Lord upon you, to bring honor to My name for more to come to Me. That they might know that the same spirit that rests in and moves through you, desires a home in them but only enters by invitation.

Matt 6:3 But when you do a charitable deed, do not let your right hand know what your left hand is doing that your charitable deed may be in secret, and your Father who sees in secret will Himself reward you openly. NKJV

Isaiah 55:1-3 "Come all you who are thirsty to the waters, come you who have no money, come, buy and eat!....I will make an everlasting covenant with you, my faithful love promised to David." NIV

John 15:7 If you abide in Me and My Words abide in you, you will ask what you desire and it shall be done for you. NKJV

Choice to Live in the Spirit

MESSAGE FROM THE LORD

There is a choice. And it is a real choice. You, by omission, will invite in the spirit of the world, the flesh or the demonic. But on purpose because of your love for Me, you purpose to invite in the Light and the Love of your heavenly nature which was promised you and breathed into you before conception, before you were conceived in your mother's womb.

Eph 2:23 "You once walked, following the course of this world, following the prince of the power of the air, the spirit that is now at work in the sons of disobedience— among whom we all once lived in the passion of the flesh." NKJV

Gen 2:7 And the LORD God formed man of the dust of the ground, and breathed into his nostrils the breath of life; and man became a living being. NKJV

Ps 139:13 For you formed my inward part. You wove me in my mother's womb. NKJV

MESSAGE FROM THE LORD

But you must again, desire and call forth your heavenly spirit to rise up and walk in this physical body that I gave you as a Temple in which I may dwell, to live and act out of your very being.

Ps 103 Bless the Lord, oh my soul; and all that is within me, bless His holy name! Bless the Lord, oh my soul, And forget not His benefits. NKJV

I Cor 6:19 Or do you know that your body is a temple of the Holy Spirit who is in you, whom you have from God, and you are not your own? NKJV

Rom 12: 1-2 I beseech you therefore brethren by the mercies of God that you present your bodies a living sacrifice, holy, acceptable to God, which is your reasonable service. And do not be conformed to this world, but be transformed by the renewing of your mind, that you may prove what is good and acceptable and perfect will of God. NKJV

MESSAGE FROM THE LORD

It's a choice. By omission, by not purposing to invite My Life and Spirit to inhabit, take residence in you, not just once but hourly, daily, moment by moment, I am shut out, and the world, the flesh and the demonic come flooding in to take up residence, to fill your thoughts, fill your desires and draw you into the winding trails away from the higher path of love and fulfillment through My Spirit resting in you.

Gal 5:16,17 I say then: Walk in the Spirit, and you shall not fulfill the lusts of the flesh against the Spirit, and the Spirit against the flesh and these are contrary to one another, so you do not do the things that you wish. NKJV

Isaiah 59:19 When the enemy comes in, like a flood the Spirit of Lord will lift up a standard against him. NKJV

MESSAGE FROM THE LORD

I bring the peace that the world cannot bring, peace that passes all understanding. The given over life, giving permission to your temple being used for its highest purpose, is a life that can then be filled with the fruits of my spirit... love, peace, joy, gentleness, goodness, kindness, patience, long suffering and self-control.

John 14:27 "Peace I leave you, My peace I give to you: not as the world gives, do I give to you. Let not your heart be troubled, neither let it be afraid."

Gal 5:22,23 But the fruit of the Spirit is love, joy, peace, long-suffering, kindness, goodness, faithfulness, gentleness, self-control. Against such there is no law. NKJV

Waiting and Trusting in God

MESSAGE FROM THE LORD

Not by your effort or by reward for your striving but by my complete grace abounding toward you. Nothing to do, but wait on Me and seek my presence, seek My face. Sing to Me as I sing over you, dance for Me as I dance over you. As your worship fills my nostrils with sweet aromas of incense of love, I pour out grace, blessings and favor.

2 Cor 9:8 And God is able to make all grace abound toward you, that you having all sufficiency in all things may have an abundance for every good work. NKJV

Ps 27:14 Wait on the LORD; Be of good courage, And He shall strengthen your heart; Wait, I say on the LORD!

Ps 27:8 When you said, "Seek My face," My heart said to You, "Your face, LORD, I will seek."

Zeph 3:17 The LORD your God in your midst, the Mighty One will save; He will rejoice over you with gladness, He will quiet you with His joy, He will rejoice over you with singing. ("rejoice" Hebraically means to dance, to spin around in joy) NKJV

Gen 8:21 And the LORD smelled a soothing aroma. Then the LORD said in His heart: "I will never again curse the ground for man's sake." KJV

MESSAGE FROM THE LORD

You must trust Me and will to trust Me in all circumstances, no matter what appearances tell you. Like faithful Job, in the end of his trial, he did not look to his friends or wife's approval; he turned to Me in faith and praised Me. All of my mighty men and women, Moses, Jeremiah, David, Elijah, Ezekiel, Peter in moments of weakness, turned away in fear and ran from me, trying to control or hide, even murder or commit adultery, but they all turned back to Me. And desired and opened to My love which I relished to pour back upon them in My mercy and kindness.

Prov 3:5 Trust in the LORD with all your heart, And lean not on your own understanding. NKJV

Acts 13:22 And when He had removed him (Saul) He raised for them, David asking, to whom He gave testimony and said, I have found David, the son of Jesse, a man after My own heart, who will do all My will. NKJV

Message From the Lord

You have no idea how much I love and desire closeness with you. I will do anything to sustain our loving intimate relationship, even release you to make mistakes so you can stumble and see that I am here to help you up. To see that I have been watching over you even and especially when you could not feel me or knew that I wept watching and waiting patiently, eager to be invited back in so I could continue and deepen the blessings I always had planned for you, before you were conceived in your mother's womb.

Isaiah 41:10 Fear not, for I am with you. Be not dismayed for I am your God. I will strengthen you. Yes I will help you, I will uphold you with My righteous right hand. NKJV

Jer 29:11 For I know the thoughts that I think toward you, says the LORD, thoughts of peace and not of evil, to give you a future and a hope. NKJV

Message From the Lord

Look to Me, seek Me and you will find Me, knock and I will enter in to reside in your heart and move in and through you. My spirit of the presence of the Lord upon you, shining so brightly that nations will rise to the light within you and kings will be drawn to the brightness of the dawn of hope within you… Me in you…the presence of the Lord upon you.

Rev 3:20 Behold I stand at the door and knock: if any one hears My voice and opens the door, I will come in to him and I will dine with him and he with Me. NKJV

Ps 18:28 For You will light my lamp; The LORD my God will enlighten my darkness. NKJV

Kingdom Glory on the Earth

MESSAGE FROM THE LORD

The seven lampstands were torched and made manifest and brought into being through the power of My word and the vision of My light shown into this world. My glory fell, the brooding of My Spirit hovering over and then the sound of my glory vibrated Life into being.

Gen 1:2 The earth was without form and void; And darkness was on the face of the deep. And the Spirit of God was hovering over the face of the waters. Then God said: "Let there be light;" and there was light. NKJV

Job 37:5 God thunders marvelously with His voice; He does great things which we cannot comprehend. NKJV

Deut 6:4 "Hear, O Israel: The LORD our God, the LORD is one." NKJV

MESSAGE FROM THE LORD

My reality then creating matter vibrating in different forms to interact and intermingle for the purpose of bringing forth a reflection, a mirror of my nature duplicated, multiplied as the sands of the sea, to create My Kingdom Glory on the earth.

Gen 1: 27 So God created man in His own image; in the image of God He created him; male and female He created them. NKJV

Gen 17: 5 No longer shall you be called Abram, but your name shall be Abraham; for I have made you a father of many nations. NKJV

Gen 22:17 indeed, I will greatly bless you and I will greatly multiply your seed as the stars of the heavens and as the sand which is on the seashore and your seed shall possess the gate of their enemies. NAS

Unity in the Spirit through Sound and Worship

MESSAGE FROM THE LORD

That one sound would resonate from people through their unified worship. That they would see that only in their breaking down all dividing walls, all misconceptions of independence, yet by My creative purpose, making each person so unique and so exquisitely perfectly themselves, they are as uniquely designed one from another as the individual snowflakes that fall from My heavens.

Ps 133: 1, 3 Behold, how good and pleasant it is, for brethren to dwell together in unity...For there the LORD commanded the blessing – Life forevermore. NKJV

1 Cor 12:12, 21 For as the body is one, and hath many members and all members of that one body, being many are one body: so also in Christ....And the eye cannot say unto the hand, I have no need of thee: nor again, the head to the feet, I have no need of you...and those members of the body which we think less honourable upon these we bestow more abundant honour....KJV

MESSAGE FROM THE LORD

So unique one from another, that their very DNA can vibrate a totally unique sound one from another so as to be actually played even in my physical realm, that when united into one sound becomes a heavenly vibration so divine that it expresses the one sound of highest divine order and reflects Me.

Ps 89:15 Blessed are the people who know the joyful sound! They walk, O LORD in the light of Your countenance. NKJV

Ps 139:14 I will praise You, for I am fearfully and wonderfully made, Marvelous are Your works, And that my soul knows very well. NKJV

Message From the Lord

Only in unity and love can the divine come forth to richly glorify Me and truly honor one another. In this unified sound of my worshipers desiring to see me and honor me, in this place do I desire to fall and rest and inhabit the praises of My people.

John 13:34 A new commandment I give to you, that you love one another, as I have loved you, that you also love one another. NKJV

Ps 22:3 But thou art holy, that inhabitest the praises of Israel. KJV (Israel includes all believers in Jesus Messiah who are grafted into the vine)

Loving each other to Sustain God's Glory

MESSAGE FROM THE LORD

Where I fall and make residence is always a place where to the degree that My glory comes into the midst of My people is the direct degree to which My people sustain an honoring of one another's uniqueness and love one another. That is loving Me the Holy Spirit within each, laying down their judgments, all accusations and limitations of thought word and deed. In this place, there is a direct correlation of the degree to which my glory can fall, rest and reside.

1 John 4:21 And this commandment we have from Him: that he who loves God must love his brother also. NKJV

Matt 7:5 Hypocrite! First remove the plank from your own eye, and then you can see clearly to remove the speck from your brother's eye. NKJV

MESSAGE FROM THE LORD

Every time I have come in what you have called revival or outpouring of My Spirit, I can only stay as long as the hearts of my people stay pure toward Me and especially toward one another as they honor Me in each of them. Fight the enemy's plan to bring forth pride, competition, strife, and every form of disunity, repenting individually and corporately anytime there is even a seed of disharmony, desiring Me more than individual recognition.

1 Cor 13: 4 – 8 Love suffers long and is kind, love does not envy; love does not parade itself, does not seek its own, is not provoked, thinks no evil; does not rejoice in iniquity, but rejoices in truth, bears all things, believes all things, hopes all things, endures all things. NKJV

Matt 18: 21-22 Then Peter came to Him and said, "Lord, how often shall my brother sin against me and I forgive him? Up to seven times?" Jesus said to him, "I do not say to you up to seven times, but up to seventy times seven." NKJV

MESSAGE FROM THE LORD

My people must fight the wiles of the enemy that would try to rob them of My glory falling and remaining. Cloud by day and fire by night is what I promise to a people who remain righteous and sanctified and consecrated unto Me and towards one another. Let My glory fall and be blessed. I so desire to bless My people. There is a commanded blessing in your remaining pure before Me and one another.

John 10:10 The thief does not come except to steal, and to kill, and to destroy. I have come that they may have life, and that they may have it more abundantly. NKJV

Exod 13:21 And the LORD went before them by day in a pillar of cloud to lead the way, and by night in a pillar of fire to give them light, so as to go by day and night. NKJV

Ps 51:10 Create in me a clean heart, O God, And renew a steadfast spirit within me. NKJV

2 Cor 10:5 casting down arguments and every high thing that exalts itself above the knowledge of God, bringing every thought into captivity to the obedience of Christ. NKJV

Seven Spirits Shining In and Through You

MESSAGE FROM THE LORD

Spirit of Wisdom and Understanding, Spirit of Counsel and Might, Spirit of Knowledge and the Fear of the Lord—these six spirits are my characteristics and aspects of Myself that reside within My nature along with the seventh being the Spirit of the Presence of the Lord upon Me, these are manifested as revelations through Light and Sound rather than through the concepts that man has attempted to apply to them. These aspects are expressions of the fullness and richness of My character.

Rev 1: 10 -16 I (John on Patmos) was in the Spirit on the LORD's Day, and I heard behind me a LOUD VOICE, as of a TRUMPET, saying "I am the Alpha and the Omega, the First and the Last,"....
Then I turned to see the VOICE that SPOKE with me. And having turned I saw SEVEN GOLDEN LAMPSTANDS, (Menorah) and in the midst of the seven lampstands (Menorah) One like the SON of MAN, clothed with a garment down to the feet and girded about the chest with a golden band. His head and hair were white like wool as white as snow, and HIS EYES like a FLAME OF FIRE; His feet were like fine brass, as if refined in a furnace, and His VOICE as the SOUND of MANY WATERS. He had in His hand SEVEN STARS, out of HIS MOUTH went a two-edged sword, and His countenance was like the SUN SHINING in its strength. NKJV

Message From the Lord

When you invite Me in, these qualities of My nature can also manifest through you, through Me who resides and dwells within you. Invite Me and My seven fold revelation of all that I Am, but I cannot and will not coexist, cohabitate with unrighteousness. That is why, when you are taken through trials and out, you count them joy knowing you are being transformed by the renewing of your minds, then you make room for Me, operating and shining in and through you.

Prov 20:27 The Spirit of a man is the lamp (menorah) of the LORD (Yahweh) searching all the innermost parts of his being. NKJV

2 Cor 6:14 Be ye not unequally yoked together with unbelievers, for what fellowship hath righteousness with unrighteousness? And what communion hath light with darkness. KJV

James 1:2, 3 My brethren, count it all joy when you fall into various trials knowing, that the testing of your faith produces patience. But let patience have its perfect work, that you may be perfect and complete, lacking nothing. NKJV

Receiving His Grace through Trials

MESSAGE FROM THE LORD

This again cannot occur by your effort, but only by grace. Only as pure gift through My Spirit so that no man can boast, but also so that you will not be destroyed when the enemy comes to rob you of your blessing.

Eph 2: 8, 9 For grace you have been saved through faith, and that not of yourselves, it is a gift of God, not of works, lest anyone should boast. NKJV

2 Cor 10:5,6 We demolish arguments and every pretension that sets itself up against the knowledge of God, and we take captive every thought to make it obedient to Christ. And we will be ready to punish every act of disobedience, once your obedience is complete. NIV

Isaiah 2:11 The eyes of the arrogant will be humbled and human pride brought low; the LORD alone will be exalted in that day. NIV

Humility and Dying to Self

MESSAGE FROM THE LORD

A series of trials which lays you low, allows opportunity after opportunity to die to self and in that suffering of the death of the old man, you are trained in the similar walk of the manifestation of walking in the sufferings of Christ. Only in this place of struck down but not destroyed, in this depth of humility is where you will surely and deeply lay hold of the Truth that the only safe tower of refuge is in the hidden place in Christ.

Phil 3:10 I want to know Christ and the power of His resurrection and the fellowship of His sufferings, being conformed to Him in His death. Berean Bible

2 Cor 4:8-10 We are hard-pressed on every side, yet not crushed.....struck down but not destroyed –always carrying about in the body the dying of the Lord Jesus, that the life of Jesus also may be manifested in our body. NKJV

Ps 91:1-2 He who dwells in the secret place of the Most High shall abide under the shadow of the Almighty. I will say of the LORD, "He is my refuge and my fortress; My God, in Him I will trust." NKJV

God's Love and Joy to Fight Your Battles

MESSAGE FROM THE LORD

The series of trials train you to know the cost and decide and commit knowing the great cost required to live for Me, resolving that you worshipping Me in you and allowing only My grace to abound toward you, can prepare you for going to the highways and byways and ultimately the nations regardless of the rejection, ridicule and persecution you will surely endure because it is not you they hate but Me in you.

2 Cor 4:16 Therefore we do not lose heart. Though outwardly we are wasting away, yet inwardly we are being renewed day by day. For our light and momentary troubles are achieving for us an eternal glory that far outweighs them all. So we fix our eyes not on what is seen but what is unseen since what is seen is temporary but what is unseen is eternal. NIV

2 Cor 9:8 And God is able to make all grace abound toward you, that you, always having all sufficiency in all things may have an abundance for every good work. NKJV

John 15:18 If the world hates you, you know that it hated me before it hated you. NKJV

Message From the Lord

For My Names Sake and for no other reason could one endure. You must know My Love and Joy that renews refreshes and resurrects Me in you to fight your battles for you over and over again. All of Me and none of you.

2 Tim 2:3 You therefore must endure hardship as a good soldier of Jesus Christ. NKJV

Ps 145:8 The LORD is gracious and compassionate, slow to anger and rich in love. NIV

Ps 16:11 You will show me the path of life; In your presence is fullness of joy; At your right hand are pleasures forevermore. NKJV

Exod 14:14 The LORD will fight for you, and you shall hold your peace. NKJV

John 15:5 I am the vine, you are the branches. He who abides in Me, and I in him, bears much fruit; for without Me you can do nothing. NKJV

MESSAGE FROM THE LORD

That you may be blessed coming in and going out, that you know you are the head and not the tail, and surely you are My Bride whom I love, an ambassador with a message from Me to those I send you to, for my higher purpose to come forth, that my harvest is gleaned. It is My heart that not one be lost and all know they are favored and My beloved children.

Deut 28:1,6 "Now it shall come to pass, if you diligently obey the voice of the LORD your God, to observe carefully all His commandments which I command you today that the LORD your God will set you high above all the nations of the earth." Blessed shall you be when you come in, and blessed shall you be when you go out. NKJV

Rev 22:17 And the Spirit and the bride say, "Come!" And let him who hears say, "Come!" And let him who thirsts come. Whoever desires let him take the water of life freely. NKJV

2 Pet 3:9 The LORD is not slack concerning His promise.....but is long-suffering toward us, not willing that any should perish but that all should come to repentance. NKJV

Seeking God's Wisdom to Live God's Way

MESSAGE FROM THE LORD

S olomon wisely asked for only wisdom, My spirit of Wisdom. He could have asked for anything but he chose that which every other treasure from My heavenly realm flows. It is Wisdom that seeks Me first and desires to embrace and live out of My awareness, walk in My ways which are not your ways.

James 3:17 But the wisdom that comes from heaven is first of all pure, then peace-loving, considerate, submissive, full of mercy and good fruit, impartial and sincere. NIV

Matt 6:1 -32 .....do not do charitable deeds before men....pray to your Father who is in the secret place...if you forgive men their trespasses, your heavenly Father will also forgive you...when you fast, do not appear to men to be fasting ....and your Father who sees in secret will reward you openly...lay up for yourselves treasures in heaven, where neither moth nor rust destroys...the lamp of your body is the eye. If therefore your eye is good, your whole body will be full of light... you cannot serve God and mammon...do not worry about your life, what you will eat or what you will drink; nor about your body, what you will put on....For your heavenly Father knows you need all these things. NKJV

Matt 6:33 But seek first the kingdom of God and His righteousness and all these things shall be added to you. NKJV

MESSAGE FROM THE LORD

Your heart is much deceived. Paul asked, "why do I do the things I do not want to do and not do the things I want to do?" The tendency of the heart due to the fallen nature of man is to be double minded. Though I still love my children, they miss the commanded blessing by wrong choices made out of foolishness, temporal lusts of the heart, immediate gratification, and shortsightedness. Without Wisdom whose plumb line is always testing choices and paths against an ultimate aim of promoting deeper peace, joy and love and then seeking My Wisdom is the key.

James 1:5-6 If any of you lacks wisdom, let him ask of God, who gives to all liberally and without reproach and it will be given him. But let him ask in faith, with no doubting, for he who doubts is like a wave of the sea driven and tossed by the wind. For let not that man suppose he will receive anything from the Lord, he is a double-minded man, unstable in all his ways. NKJV

MESSAGE FROM THE LORD

The only true wisdom must be sought from a place of seeking the heart of Wisdom of the Holy Spirit. I come to make a home in you to guide you in all things. I am compelled by your heart of surrender to desire My ways to direct you that you are blessed in all things.

John 14: 15 -18 "If you love Me, keep My commandments. And I will pray the Father and He will give you another Helper, that He may abide with you forever—the Spirit of truth whom the world cannot receive, for He dwells with you and will be in you. I will not leave you orphans, I will come to you." NKJV

John 14: 21, 23 "He who has My commandments and keeps them it is he who loves Me: And he who loves Me will be loved by My Father, and I will love him, and manifest Myself to him"..."If anyone love Me, he will keep My word; and My Father will love him, and we will come to him and make Our home with him." NKJV

Following God's Direction in All Things

MESSAGE FROM THE LORD

A s you sow so shall you reap, and in your unraveled transparent love and uninhibited willingness to follow My direction, your faith walk and obedience draws out from within Me, exuding then through you My Wisdom to hear and then follow the wise course in all your dealings in relationships, finances, destiny and all matters of the heart big and small.

Gal 6:7 Do not be deceived, God is not mocked; for whatever a man sows, that he will also reap. *NKJV*

Ps 37: 3-4 Trust in the LORD, and do good; Dwell in the land, and feed on His faithfulness. Delight yourself also in the LORD, And He shall give you the desires of your heart. *NKJV*

Isaiah 30:21 Your ears shall hear a word behind you saying, "This is the way, walk in it," Whenever you turn to the right hand Or whenever you turn to the left. *NKJV*

John 8:32 "And you shall know the truth, and the truth shall make you free." *NKJV*

John 10:27 "My sheep hear My voice and I know them, and they follow Me." *NKJV*

John 13:16 However, when He the Spirit of truth has come, He will guide you into all truth; for He will not speak on His own authority, but whatever He hears He will speak; and He will tell you things to come. *NKJV*

MESSAGE FROM THE LORD

"Follow Me" meant follow me in thought, word and deed. Let My ways be your ways. If you seek My ways, they are Ways of Wisdom that lead to blessing for you and anyone in your sphere of influence. Your sphere of influence then grows as you are faithful to follow my wise counsel in small matters, then I know I can trust you in larger arenas and venues.

Matthew 16:24-26 Then Jesus said to His disciples, "If anyone wishes to come after Me, he must deny himself, and take up his cross and follow Me." For whoever wishes to save his life will lose it, but whoever loses his life for My sake will find it." For what will it profit a man if he gains the whole world and forfeits his soul? Or what will a man give in exchange for his soul? NKJV

Luke 18:28-30 Peter said, "Behold, we have left our homes and followed You." And He (Jesus) said to them, "Truly I say to you, there is no one who has left house or wife or brothers or parents or children, for the sake of the Kingdom of God, who will not receive many times as much at this time and in the age to come, eternal life." NKJV

Ps 37:34 "Wait on the LORD, and keep His way and He shall exalt you to inherit the land." NKJV

Ps 128:1-2 Blessed are all who fear the LORD who walk in obedience to him. You will eat the fruit of your labor; blessings and prosperity will be yours. NIV

1 Chron 4:10 And Jabez called on the God of Israel saying, "Oh, that You would bless me indeed, and enlarge my territory, that Your hand would be with me, and that You would keep me from evil, that I may not cause pain!" So God granted him what he requested. NKJV

Trusting God and Resting in Him

MESSAGE FROM THE LORD

Trust Me and wait on Me to hear My voice. My sheep know My voice because we are so intimate and have spent so much time together that My voice cannot be mistaken for another's. A close friend's voice or laughter can be picked out in a large crowd, so is it with Me.

John 10:27-28 My sheep hear My voice, and I know them, and they shall never perish, neither shall anyone snatch them out of My hand. NKJV

Deut 28:2 And all these blessings shall come upon you and overtake you, because you obey the voice of the LORD your God. NKJV

John 14:26 But the Helper, the Holy Spirit, whom the Father will send in My name, He will teach you all things and bring to your remembrance all things. NKJV

Matt 4:4 Man shall not live by bread alone, but by every word that proceeds from the mouth of God. NKJV

MESSAGE FROM THE LORD

Rest in Me, draw close to Me that I may know you and you--Me, deeper still. Be still and know that I am God.

Matt 11:28-30 "Come to Me, all you who labor and are heavy laden, and I will give you rest. Take My yoke upon you and learn from Me, for I am gentle and lowly in heart, and you will find rest for your souls. For My yoke is easy and My burden is light." NKJV

Ps 46:10-11 Be still, and know that I am God; I will be exalted among the nations, I will be exalted in the earth! The LORD of hosts is with us; The God of Jacob is our refuge. NKJV

Walking in the Spirits of Wisdom and Understanding

MESSAGE FROM THE LORD

I reveal understanding in matters from the heart of My compassion. I always show you how to kiss mercy with justice. Many of My people know Truth but must counsel with My Spirit to gain the perspective of a merciful response.

Ps 85:10 Mercy and truth are met together, righteousness and peace have kissed each other. KJV

Zech 7:9 "Thus has the LORD of hosts said, 'Dispense true justice and practice kindness and compassion each to his brother.' NAS

Col 3:12-14 So, as those who have been chosen of God, holy and beloved, put on a heart of compassion, kindness, humility, gentleness and patience; bearing with one another, and forgiving each other, whoever has a complaint against anyone; just as the LORD forgave you, so also should you. Beyond all these things put on love, which is the perfect bond of unity. NAS

MESSAGE FROM THE LORD

One can hear wisdom and truth about someone but without My Spirit of understanding, which offers love and forgiveness and blesses rather than shames or condemns, one's tongue can be used to curse rather than bless.

Isa 35:3-4 Strengthen the weak hands, and make firm the feeble knees. Say to those who have an anxious heart, "Be strong; fear not! Behold, your God will come with vengeance, with the recompense of God. He will come and save you." ESV

John 3:17 For God did not send his Son into the world to condemn the world but in order that the world might be saved through him. ESV

Rom 8:1 There is therefore now no condemnation for those who are in Christ Jesus. ESV

Message From the Lord

Wisdom and Understanding must always operate in alliance and balance with one another so that you or another are lifted up, encouraged to rise up in their spirit man and go higher to a place of their highest calling and destiny, calling one up to be the person that I made them to be.

Rom 15: 1-3 We who are strong ought to bear with the failings of the weak and not please ourselves. Each of us should please our neighbors for their good to build them up. For even Christ did not please himself, but as it is written, "The insults of those who insult you have fallen on me." NIV

Rom 14:19 Therefore let us pursue the things which make for peace and the things by which one may edify another. NKJV

1 Cor 14: 1-3 Pursue love, and earnestly desire the spiritual gifts especially that you may prophesy. For one who speaks in a tongue speaks not to men but to God...On the other hand, the one who prophecies speaks to people for their upbuilding and encouragement and consolation. ESV

MESSAGE FROM THE LORD

All can only live the kingdom life, accessing and living out of the queenly kingly kingdom reality if they are entering as children. How do we treat and encourage a child?—with tender wisdom coupled with understanding.

Gal 4:6-7 And because you are sons, God has sent forth the Spirit of His Son into your hearts, crying out, "Abba Father!" Therefore you are no longer a slave but a son, and if a son then an heir of God through Christ. NKJV

Rev 5:10 You have made them to be a kingdom and priests to serve our God, and they will reign on the earth. NIV

Matt 19:14 Jesus said, "Let the children come to me and do not hinder them, for the kingdom of heaven belongs to such as these. NIV

Matt 18:4 Therefore whoever humbles himself as this little child is greatest in the kingdom of heaven. NKJV

MESSAGE FROM THE LORD

In all your ways acknowledge Me and I will make your path straight but only if you consult with the Spirit of Wisdom and Understanding that lives within you. Search Me and you will find the Pearl of Great Price.

Prov 3:5-6 Trust in the LORD with all your heart, And lean not on your own understanding; In all your ways acknowledge Him, And He shall direct your paths. NKJV

Matt 13:45-46 Again, the kingdom of heaven is like a merchant seeking beautiful pearls, who, when he had found one pearl of great price, went and sold all that he had and bought it. NKJV

Inviting and Receiving the Spirits of Counsel and Might

MESSAGE FROM THE LORD

The request from you and invitation from Me to receive a revelation of My Spirit of Counsel and Might will allow My supernatural grace for boldness to speak to people, leaders—whether they be leaders in business, education, politics, or kings and queens of nations.

Exod 8:16 "But I have raised you up for this very purpose, that I might show you my power and that my name might be proclaimed to all the earth." NIV

I Chron 16:24 "Declare his glory among the nations, his marvelous deeds among all peoples." NIV

Message From the Lord

Your heart will faint at the very thought of such encounters when attempting these interactions with individuals of influence without My Spirit of Counsel and Might resting on you by My indwelling Spirit. The enemy of your soul and the demonic realm is tenacious in this war to battle against a saint who desires to bring light into the dark hidden places of this world.

Acts 26:16 -18 But rise and stand on your feet for I have appeared to you for this purpose, to make you a minister and a witness…to open their eyes, in order to turn them from darkness to light and the power of satan to God….NKJV

I John 2:27 But the anointing which you received from Him abides in you, and you do not need that anyone teach you concerning all things, and is true, and is not a lie, just as it has taught you, you will abide in Him. NKJV

Isa 40:31 But those who wait upon the LORD shall renew their strength; they shall mount up with wings like eagles, they shall run and not be weary, they shall walk and not faint. NKJV

God's Might to Walk in His Courage

MESSAGE FROM THE LORD

Satan does not give up territory without a fight, so you must be flying under the radar or soaring with me in the Spirit above the cloud of darkness with the full ammunition of the glory resting on you. By calling on Me, allowing ample time to rest in Me for hours, days and weeks at a time, to allow a proper filling and overshadowing of My Spirit then you may walk into a place where you are to bring My wise counsel to individuals of influence with a clear message from Me or revelation that I have directed.

Ps 91:1,9-10 He who dwells in the secret place of the Most High shall abide under the shadow of the Almighty.... Because you have made the LORD, who is my refuge, even the Most High, your dwelling place, No evil shall befall you...
NKJV

Jer 1:8 "Do not be afraid of their faces, for I am with you to deliver you," says the LORD. NKJV

MESSAGE FROM THE LORD

Like reading from a scroll, you will be operating out of great grace abounding toward you to deliver the decree—revelation, interpretation, and application that requires great courage.

Jer 36:6 You go therefore, and read from the scroll which you have written at my instruction, the words of the LORD, in the hearing of the people of the LORD's house on the day of fasting. NKJV

2 Cor 9:8 And is able to make all grace abound toward you, that you always having all sufficiency in all things; may have an abundance for every good work. NKJV

Message From the Lord

No fear can enter in so you need the Spirit of Counsel coupled with my Great Might to deliver the direction with authority and power. As I, the Lion of Judah is invited to roar through you, rising up from the great deep well of Me resting in you, you will trample on lions and cobras and overcome the fear that your flesh man could only cower and back off from.

Isaiah 40:20 He gives power to the weak, and to those who have no might He increases strength. NKJV

Rev 5:5 But one of the elders said to me (John), "Do not weep. Behold, the Lion of the tribe of Judah, the Root of David, has prevailed to open the scroll and to loose its seven seals." NKJV

Hosea 11:10 They shall walk after the LORD. He will roar like a lion. When He roars then His sons shall come trembling from the west....NKJV

Intimacy with God to Walk in Your Calling

MESSAGE FROM THE LORD

Rising up in the flesh to convey a message leaves My beloved wounded and disheartened and destroyed. Rest and prepare in and under My Glory for the great day of My purposes and plans to come forth drawing on My Spirit of Counsel and Might for My honor and My glory with great humility submitting and surrendering, desiring no fame or fortune., only to bless the Father and My Spirit resting within you. Remember your treasures are in heaven.

Ps 27:14 Wait on the LORD, Be of good courage, And He shall strengthen your heart; Wait, I say, on the LORD! NKJV

Eph 4:1,2 As a prisoner for the LORD, then, I urge you to live a life worthy of the calling you have received. Be completely humble and gentle, be patient, bearing one another in love. NIV

Matt 6:20,21 but lay up for yourselves treasures in heaven, where neither moth nor rust destroys and where thieves do not break in and steal. For where your treasure is, there your heart will be also. NKJV

MESSAGE FROM THE LORD

My Spirit of Counsel will guide not only in the exact message, I will guide you in the specific time and place, bringing about divine appointments. I will reveal strategies and warn you against pitfalls, dangers and potential retaliations.

Acts 20:27 "I did not shrink from declaring to you the whole counsel of God." ESV

Ps 33:10-11 The LORD brings the counsel of the nations to nothing; he frustrates the plans of the peoples. The counsel of the LORD stands forever, the plans of His heart to all generations. ESV

Ps 37:23 "The steps of a good man are ordered of the LORD, And He delights in his way. NKJV

MESSAGE FROM THE LORD

All of this requires great discernment, submission, surrender and that comes through intimacy with Me. Great grace must abound toward you in all circumstances so the cost of delivering one crucial message or taking a courageous action might require a preparation of a lifetime of intimacy that I may know that My beloved is so submitted they will not be hurt if I send them out on an important mission.

1 Peter 5: 6-7 Therefore humble yourselves under the mighty hand of God, that He may exalt you in due time, casting all your care upon Him, for He cares for you. NKJV

Josh 1:7 Be strong and very courageous. Be careful to obey all the law my servant Moses gave you; do not turn from it to the right or to the left, that you may be successful wherever you go. NIV

John 15:5 "I am the vine, you are the branches, He who abides in Me, and I in him, bears much fruit, for without Me you can do nothing."

MESSAGE FROM THE LORD

Prepare in the intimacy of My chambers as My Bride, My Warrior Bride, My readied soldier, who knows she or he must put on the armor and let Me fight the battle, confident of the victory because I am the Lion of Judah walking shoulder to shoulder with the slain lamb within you as a humbled yet courageous servant.

James 4:8 "Draw near to God, and he will draw near to you." NKJV

Eph 6:10-13 Finally be strong in the LORD and in his mighty power. Put on the full armor of God, so you can take a stand against the devil's schemes. For our struggle is not against flesh and blood, but against the rulers, against the authorities, against the powers of this dark world, and against the spiritual forces of evil in the heavenly realms. NIV

MESSAGE FROM THE LORD

Then sent by Me, you will enter like a glory bomb to explode the good news into the face of darkness erupting light to violently and suddenly eradicate darkness, dramatically and eternally changing the tide of earthly events.

Deut 20:4 "For the LORD your God is the one who goes with you to fight for you against your enemies to give you victory," NIV

Eph 6:14-16 Therefore, put on the full armor of God, so when the day of evil comes you may be able to stand your ground and after you have done everything, to stand. Stand firm... with the belt of truth...breastplate of righteousness....feet fitted....in the gospel of peace...shield of faith...helmet of salvation and sword of the Spirit which is the word of God. NIV

Matt 11:12 And from the days of John the Baptist until now the kingdom of heaven suffers violence, and the violent take it by force. NKJV

Message From the Lord

Be prepared….be prepared …in intimacy with Me and My Spirit of Counsel and Might within you.

Jer 33:3 'Call to Me, and I will answer you, and show you great and mighty things, which you do not know.' NKJV

Jer 29:11 For I know the thoughts I think toward you, says the LORD, thoughts of peace and not evil, to give you a future and a hope. Then you will call upon Me and go and pray to Me, and I will listen to you. And you will seek Me and find Me, when you search for Me with all your heart. NKJV

Balancing Knowledge and Fear of the Lord

MESSAGE FROM THE LORD

Revelation knowledge from the Tree of Life is directly opposed to the facts drawn from the Knowledge of the Tree of Good and Evil.

Rev 2:7 He who has an ear, let him hear what the Spirit says to the churches. To him who overcomes, I will give to eat of the tree of life, which is in the midst of the Paradise of God. NKJV

Gen 2: 8-9 The LORD God planted a garden eastward of Eden, and there He put the man whom He had formed. And out of the ground the LORD God made every tree grow that is pleasant to the sight and good for food. The tree of life was also in the midst of the garden and the tree of the knowledge of good and evil. NKJV

MESSAGE FROM THE LORD

The spirit realm of the dark and light can both be tapped however drawing revelation from My Spirit which rests upon you through My Glory, not by your might or power but by My Spirit, is pure revelation that testifies and witnesses to My Spirit and edifies, comforts, strengthens giving interpretation and application that can only come from one's Creator whose purpose and plan is to strengthen the bond between God and man and bring hope and furtherance of an individual's true high calling.

John 15:26 But when the Helper comes, whom I shall send to you from the Father, the Spirit of truth who proceeds from the Father, He will testify of Me. NKJV

1 Cor 14:1,3 Pursue love and desire spiritual gifts but especially that you may prophecy. But he who prophecies speaks to men for their edification, encouragement, and comfort. NKJV

Phil 3:14 I press toward the goal for the prize of the upward call of God in Christ Jesus. NKJV

MESSAGE FROM THE LORD

The psychic occult realm can bring information even some superficial correct information about an individual's life because it taps the spiritual airwaves which is open to all, however the occult provides a counterfeit to the high plan of God and draws My beloved into false idolatry.

Isaiah 44:24-25 This is what the LORD says --- your Redeemer, who formed you in the womb: I am the LORD, the Maker of all things, who stretches out the heavens, who spreads out the earth by myself, who foils the signs of the false prophets, and makes fools of diviners, who overthrows the learning of the wise and turns it into nonsense. NIV

Acts 16:16-18 Once when we were going to the place of prayer, we were met by a female slave who had a spirit by which she predicted the future. She earned a great deal of money for her owners by fortune-telling. She followed Paul and the rest of us shouting, "These men are servants of the Most High God, who are telling you the way to be saved." She kept this up for days. Finally Paul became so annoyed that he turned around and said to the spirit, "In the name of Jesus Christ I command you to come out of her!" At that moment the spirit left her. NIV

MESSAGE FROM THE LORD

Those spirits tapping the knowledge of the Tree of the Knowledge of Good and Evil will, by its intent, draw one's reliance and focus away from intimacy and deeper relationship with Me and even undermine belief and leaning on one's Creator. My Spirit of Knowledge and the Spirit of the Fear of the Lord go hand and hand because one who is surrendered and submitted to My will is operating in holy reverence and awe of Me.

Prov 3:7 Do not be wise in your own eyes; Fear the LORD and depart from evil. NKJV

Prov 14:27 The fear of the LORD is a fountain of life, To turn one away from the snares of death. NKJV

Prov 9:10 The fear of the LORD is the beginning of wisdom, And the knowledge of the Holy One is understanding. NKJV

MESSAGE FROM THE LORD

To the degree that one is bowed in trembling reverence before his Lord to want to hear only and specifically from Me and My Spirit for oneself or another, when one seeks My Knowledge with holy fear through the Spirit of the Fear of the Lord, then they will wait on Me before acting or speaking into situations.

Prov 15:33 The fear of the LORD is the instruction of wisdom, And before honor is humility. NKJV

Deut 13:4 You shall follow the LORD your God and fear Him, and you shall keep His commandments, listen to His voice, serve Him and cling to Him. NKJV

MESSAGE FROM THE LORD

Knowledge received must be submitted and resubmitted to Me, from that place of reverential awe and trembling so that one does not intermingle one's own flesh or allow personal ambition or pride to influence or distort the word or direction assumed to be heard of Me.

1 John 4:1-3 Beloved, do not believe every spirit, but test the spirits, whether they are of God, because many false prophets have gone out into the world. By this you know the Spirit of God: Every spirit that confesses that Jesus Christ has come in the flesh is of God, and every spirit that does not confess that Jesus Christ has come in the flesh is not of God. And this is the spirit of the Antichrist, which you have heard was coming, and is now already in the world. NKJV

Phil 2:3 Do not act out of selfish ambition or conceit, but with humility think of others as being better than yourselves. NKJV

All Honor and Glory to God to Bear Fruit

MESSAGE FROM THE LORD

A surrendered life bringing forth the fruit of holiness, purity and righteousness must be at the core of one's character. Only one purpose and motive must be the guiding force which is to seek honor and glory for Me and Me alone, your Savior, your Beloved, your Creator and your King.

Eph 4:20 You have not so learned Christ, if indeed you have heard Him and have been taught by Him, as the truth is in Jesus: that you put off, concerning your former conduct, the old man which grows corrupt according to the deceitful lusts, and be renewed in the spirit of your mind, and that you put on the new man which was created according to God, in true righteousness and holiness. NKJV

Rev 4:11 "You are worthy, our Lord and God to receive glory and honor and power, for you created all things; and by your will they were created and have their being," NIV

Message From The Lord

You are to bring honor and glory to My Name and to feed and draw my sheep closer to Me. Then I can bear fruit that will last in and through this Temple that has submitted and surrendered his or her life for My Glory and Honor.

John 21:17 The third time he (Jesus) said to him, "Simon son of John, do you love me?" Peter was hurt because Jesus asked him the third time. "Do you love me?" He said, "LORD you know all things; you know that I love you." Jesus said, "Feed my sheep." NIV

Rom 12:1-2 I beseech you therefore, brethren by the mercies of God, that you present your bodies a living sacrifice, holy acceptable to God, which is your reasonable service. And do not be conformed to this world, but be transformed by the renewing of your mind, that you may prove what is that good and acceptable and perfect will of God. NKJV

MESSAGE FROM THE LORD

And those who go low, I will lift up and uphold them with my righteous right hand and bring unmerited favor toward them by their willingness to lay low, stay hidden in Me that I might be revealed to My Flock.

1Peter 5:5-6....."God resists the proud, But gives grace to the humble." Therefore humble yourselves under the mighty hand of God, that He may exalt you in due time. NKJV

Ps 91:1-4 He who dwells in the secret place of the Most High shall abide under the shadow of the Almighty. I will say of the LORD, "He is my refuge and my fortress; My God, in Him I will trust." Surely He shall deliver you from the snare of the fowler, And from the perilous pestilence. He shall cover you with His feathers, And under His wings you shall take refuge; His truth shall be your shield and buckler. NKJV

Dedication

To Him be all Glory
and Honor who is the
True Author and Finisher
of His Work
forming us into vessels
worthy of our calling
to shine His
Light that He may
be seen and
Loved as we are Loved
by Him.